AF361836

For Kailani and Alva.

And for an endangered species:

Those who feel their true calling and
have the courage to follow it.

ARUN AND RUNA

we are nature

Text
Valérie Grüninger

Illustration
Nicole DeBarber

Runa and her big friend Arun, the Dragon, have been friends for as long as they can remember.

They share the same home and love where they live...

Maybe just like you!

Arun is clever and knows a lot.

Runa likes that because she has many questions.

"Arun, do you know why my ears are round
and not as pointy as yours?"
Runa wants to know from her best friend.

"Your body is full of wonders.
You have a lot in common with your home, the Earth.
Climb on my back, and I'll show you," Arun says.

While she listens to the sound of the waves and the distant approaching storm, Runa asks,

"Do you know why my tears taste salty?"

"Your tears are meant to always remind you of the sea," Arun answers.

"The ocean is wild and wonderful, just like you."

"I am afraid of the thunder, Arun. Let's go back,"
shouts Runa through the heavy wind.

Arun answers steadfastly,
"Lightning is power made visible.
You have a lot in common with it.

Your veins have the
same shape.

There is a lot of energy running through your body.
You are very powerful."

"I don't only have veins on my wrist, but also beauty marks.

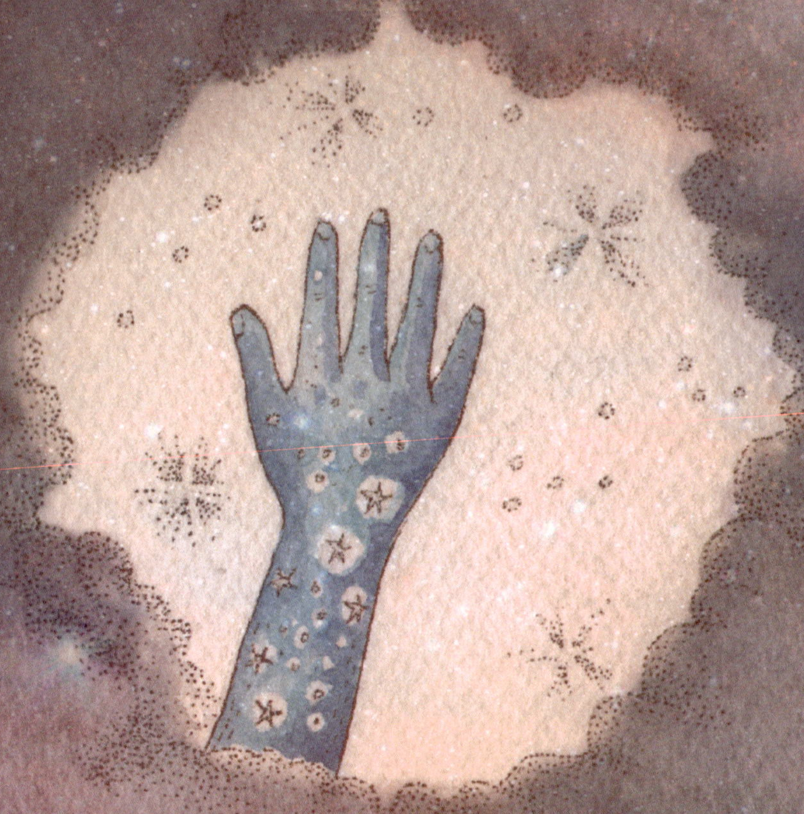

So, what are they good for then, Arun?"

"They are meant to remind you of the stars in the sky," he implies.

"But not only your freckles, but also your..."

"…your eyes.

Your eye color and
the beauty marks on
your skin are unique.

Just like the stars,
you are also unique and
perfect just the way you are."

"Arun, why can I open and close my eyes?" Runa asks.

"In nature, there is day and night," Arun answers.
"There are things that can be felt better in the dark.
Some things are seen better in daylight."

"Our emotions are often revealed to us clearly
when it's dark and quiet because the
darkness invites us to take a look inside.
Never be afraid of your feelings, Runa."

"Arun, why can I hear my heart beating?".
Runa asks.

"Your heart is like a compass," Arun explains.

"When it beats loudly, it's trying to share a message with you—for example, that something is unusual or maybe exceptionally beautiful."

"Wow, my heart is like a trusted friend whispering to me!" Runa exclaims.

"Absolutely! It's just like nature itself, whispering to us always—in still and wild rhythms—if only we have the courage to listen," Arun adds.

In the forest, a cool breeze brushes through Runa's
hair, and she gasps, "The wind…"

"…is like the breath of the Earth," Arun adds.
"Breathing means being alive. It's said that trees are the lungs
of the Earth. That's why it's no coincidence that your lungs
resemble this canopy of trees."

Runa takes a deep breath
and responds,

"It seems that humans and
trees have much in common."

"Trees are like old friends," Arun says.
"Some have been here for hundreds of years.

Your skin is a lot like their bark. As trees get older, their surface
changes. And just like trees, our skin transforms as we grow older.
It's nature's way of showing the beauty of time."

Runa marvels and says,
"You are right. This tree could be my grandmother.
My granny's skin looks the same."

"What do I have in common with a river, Arun?"

"Well, imagine your blood as a gentle river, flowing through you and nourishing your entire being. It carries important things through your body, just like water nourishes the nature surrounding you," Arun explains.

"That's so well thought out. Everything in life is part of a great cycle," Runa realizes.

"Arun, you forgot about the ears!
What do my ears have in common with nature?"
Runa asks excitedly.

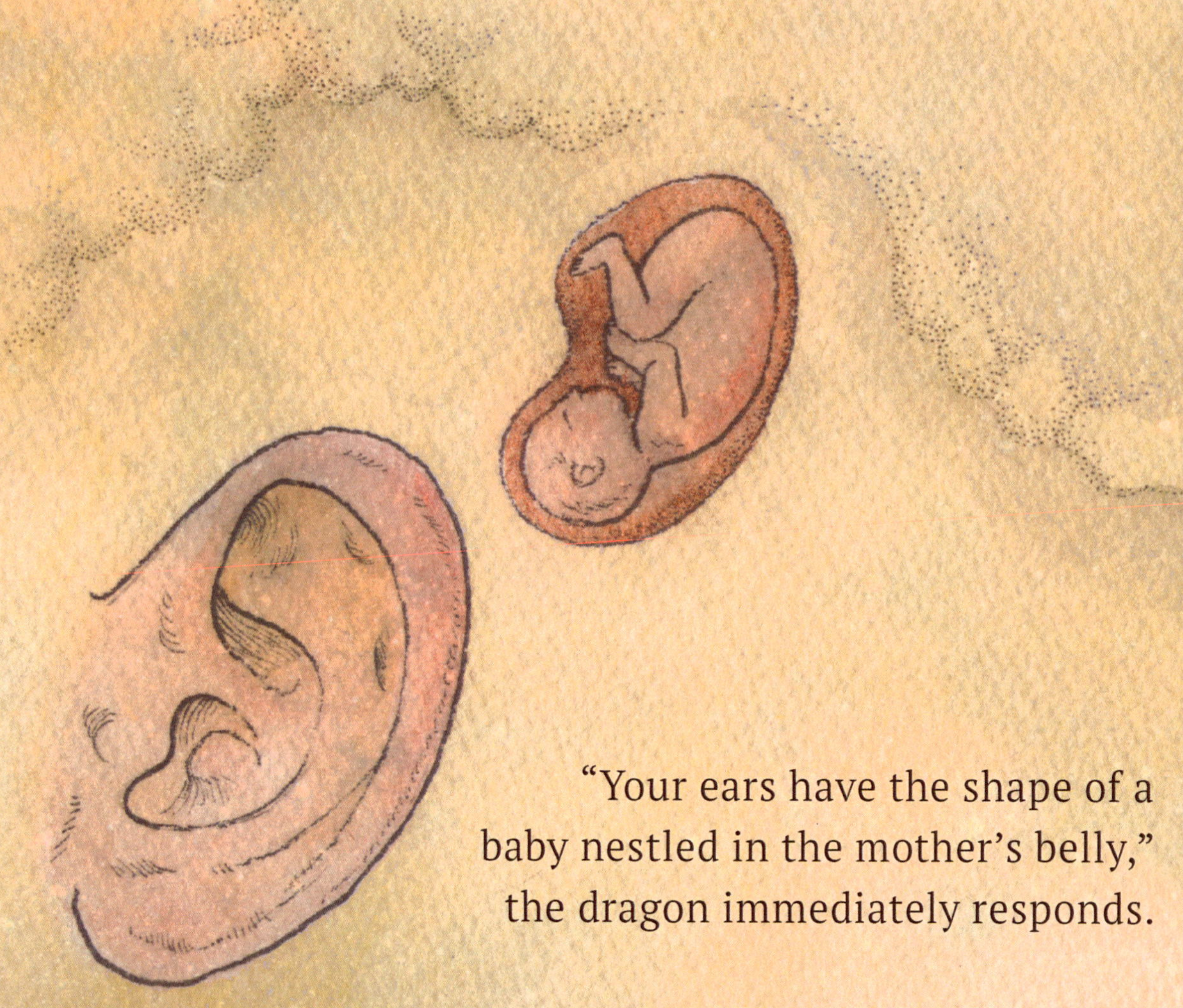

"Your ears have the shape of a
baby nestled in the mother's belly,"
the dragon immediately responds.

"It's meant to remind you of how small you once
were and how much you are capable of now."

"That's right, today I am big and brave,"
Runa rejoices.

Suddenly, it becomes dark, and Runa whispers,

"My home and I, the Earth, have many things in common.

Thank you, Arun, for showing
them to me."

A deep tiredness overcomes the girl.

The dragon leans over his friend and
whispers in a gentle voice:

"You are a unique, wonderful, wise, and courageous human being, Runa."

Zzz

"Should you ever forget," he adds softly,
"let nature remind you of how wonderful you are.
Take care of your home, for you and it
are very much alike."

ARUN AND RUNA
we are nature

Text
Valérie Grüninger

Illustration
Nicole DeBarber
www.linktr.ee/NicoleDeBarber

Graphic Design
Myriam Roy

1st edition 2024
ISBN (Hardcover) 978-3-9525892-9-8
ISBN (Softcover) 978-3-9525892-8-1

*For information or to reproduce selections of this book,
write to **info@sacredways.ch***

9 783952 589298